D1518486

Animal 911
ENVIRONMENTAL THREATS

The Threat of Invasive Species

KAREN O'CONNOR

Gareth Stevens
Publishing

Please visit our website, www.garethstevens.com
For a free color catalog of all our high-quality books,
call toll free 1-800-542-2595 or fax 1-877-542-2596.

Library of Congress Cataloging-in-Publication Data

O'Connor, Karen.
The threat of invasive species / by Karen O'Connor.
  p. cm. -- (Animal 911: environmental threats)
Includes index.
ISBN 978-1-4339-9723-5 (pbk.)
ISBN 978-1-4339-9724-2 (6-pack)
ISBN 978-1-4339-9722-8 (library binding)
1. Biological invasions—Juvenile literature. 2. Nonindigenous pests—Juvenile literature. I. Title.
QH353.O35 2014
577.18—dc23

First Edition

Published in 2014 by
Gareth Stevens Publishing
111 East 14th Street, Suite 349
New York, NY 10003

Produced by Planman Technologies
Designed by Sandy Kent
Edited by Jon Bogart

Photo credits: Cover(t): xpixel/Shutterstock.com; Cover(b): Neil Burton/Shutterstock.com; Background : LeksusTuss/
Shutterstock.com; Inside: Pg 4: Srijan Roy Choudhury/Shutterstock.com; Pg 5: ©tbkmedia.de/Alamy/IndiaPicture; Pg 6:
©Nigel Cattlin/Alamy/IndiaPicture; Pg 7(t): Volodymyr Burdiak/Shutterstock.com; Pg 7(b): Matt Jeppson/Shutterstock.
com; Pg 8: StudioNewmarket/Shutterstock.com; Pg 9(t): ©Dan Callister/Alamy/IndiaPicture; Pg 9(b): Blanscape/
Shutterstock.com; Pg 10: ©Islandstock/Alamy/IndiaPicture; Pg 11(t): David P. Lewis/Shutterstock.com; Pg 11(b): ©FLPA/
Alamy/IndiaPicture; Pg 12: ©aaron peterson.net/Alamy/IndiaPicture; Pg 13: Fotokostic/Shutterstock.com; Pg 14:
slavik65/Shutterstock.com; Pg 15(t): Analia Valeria Urani/Shutterstock.com; Pg 15(b): StevenRussellSmithPhotos/
Shutterstock.com; Pg 16: SweetCrisis/Shutterstock.com; Pg 17: ©Nigel Cattlin/Alamy/IndiaPicture; Pg 18: Martynova
Anna/Shutterstock.com; Pg 19(t): siloto/Shutterstock.com; Pg 19(b): Lee Prince/Shutterstock.com; Pg 20: ©imagebroker/
Alamy/IndiaPicture; Pg 21: Laurie L. Snidow/Shutterstock.com; Pg 22: Daniel Prudek/Shutterstock.com; Pg 23(l): Jens
Metschurat/Shutterstock.com; Pg 23(r): Markus Gann/Shutterstock.com; Pg 24(t): National Geography/IndiaPicture;
Pg 24(b): Venus Angel/Shutterstock.com; Pg 25: Brian Lasenby/Shutterstock.com; Pg 26: ©Robert McGouey/Wildlife/
Alamy/IndiaPicture; Pg 27: ©Amazon-Images/Alamy/IndiaPicture; Pg 28(l): Dirk Ercken/Shutterstock.com; Pg 28(r):
Rufous/Shutterstock.com; Pg 29(t): Torsten Lorenz/Shutterstock.com; Pg 29(b): Neil Burton/Shutterstock.com;
Pg 30: ©David Chapman/Alamy/IndiaPicture; Pg 31: ©John T.L/Alamy/IndiaPicture; Pg 32(t): Photoshot/IndiaPicture;
Pg 32(b): ©E.R. Degginger/Alamy/IndiaPicture; Pg 33: Janelle Lugge/Shutterstock.com; Pg 34: ©William Mullins/Alamy/
IndiaPicture; Pg 35: altanaka/Shutterstock.com; Pg 36: ©Jason Lindsey/Alamy/IndiaPicture; Pg 37: ©Jim O Donnell/
Alamy/IndiaPicture; Pg 38: ©Jim O Donnell/Alamy/IndiaPicture; Pg 39: Erick Margarita Images/Shutterstock.com; Pg 40:
itay uri/Shutterstock.com; Pg 41: southmind/Shutterstock.com; Pg 42: ©John Cancalosi/Alamy/IndiaPicture; Pg 43:
Loop/IndiaPicture; Pg 44: scubaluna/Shutterstock.com; Pg 45: Sergey Uryadnikov/Shutterstock.com.

t=Top, b=Bottom, l=Left, r=Right

Printed in the United States of America

CPSIA compliance information: Batch #CS13GS. For further information contact Gareth Stevens, New York, New York at
1-800-542-2595.

Contents

Words in the glossary appear in **bold** type the first time they are used in the text.

What Is an Invasive Species?

What if strangers moved into your house and ate all your food? Your family would be in danger.

Something like this happens in the animal kingdom. Animals that take over the food and **habitats** of other animals are called **invasive species**. Invasive species are good fighters. They eat whatever they can find. They create large families in a short time. Unfortunately for **native species**, invasive species do not have natural **predators** to keep them under control.

Red-vented bulbuls, like this one, are an invasive species.

A flock of European starlings like this one can do great damage to a field.

The European starling is one of these invaders. This bird came to the United States from Europe over a century ago. European starlings fly in huge flocks. When one bird gives the signal, the flock lifts off the ground. Some flocks are so large they blacken the sky.

It is a sight to see. But what people may not see is that these birds are **pests**. They eat animal feed and carry diseases. They steal nesting sites from other birds. European starlings cost farmers more than $800 million a year.

World Threat

Invasive species hurt **wildlife**. The grey squirrel spreads disease to the red squirrel.

Rats from Asia harm the mohua, or yellowhead bird, in New Zealand.

Rodents in South America dig under water plants and eat their roots. They kill the plants and ruin the habitats of many bird species.

The boll weevil, which feeds on cotton buds, came from Mexico to the United States over 100 years ago. It devastated cotton farms throughout the South. This pest costs cotton farmers over $50 billion a year.

Boll weevils, like the one shown here, are destructive pests.

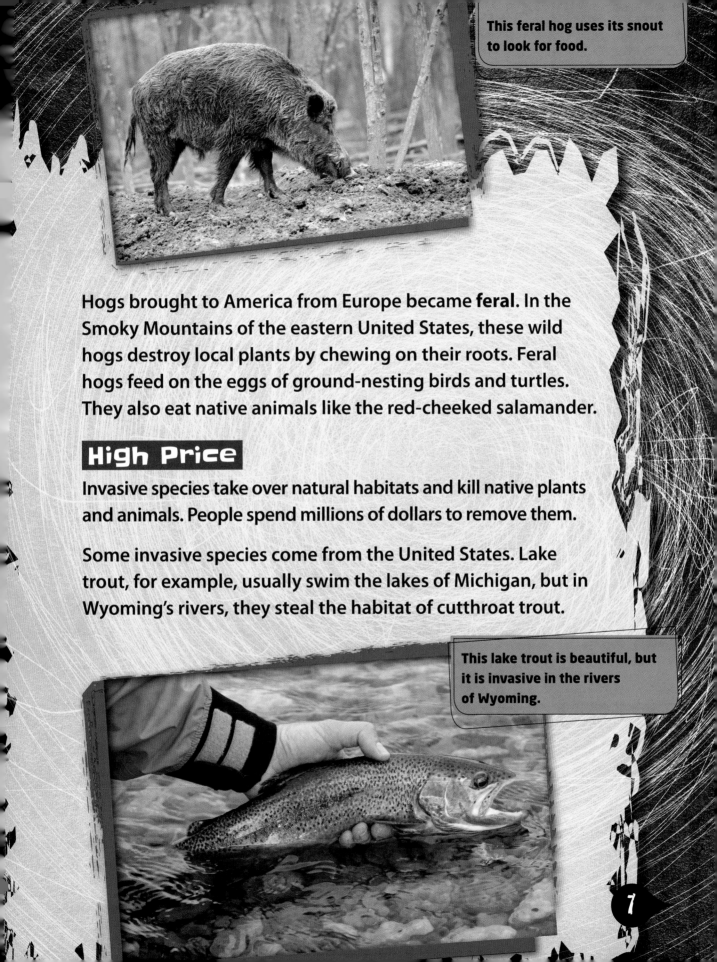

This feral hog uses its snout to look for food.

Hogs brought to America from Europe became **feral**. In the Smoky Mountains of the eastern United States, these wild hogs destroy local plants by chewing on their roots. Feral hogs feed on the eggs of ground-nesting birds and turtles. They also eat native animals like the red-cheeked salamander.

High Price

Invasive species take over natural habitats and kill native plants and animals. People spend millions of dollars to remove them.

Some invasive species come from the United States. Lake trout, for example, usually swim the lakes of Michigan, but in Wyoming's rivers, they steal the habitat of cutthroat trout.

This lake trout is beautiful, but it is invasive in the rivers of Wyoming.

Causes of Invasion

Invasive species are in water, on land, and in the air. They come by boat, airplane, and wind from their homelands. They attack wildlife, natural areas, and farms. There are many ways for invaders to hitch a ride to a new location.

Transport

Insects and mice tag along in boxes loaded onto ships, trucks, cars, and trains. When these animals reach a new location, they grab food and habitats from the native species. In a short time, the area is changed for the worse.

Tiny insects make great invaders. They destroy forests, eat crops, and spread disease.

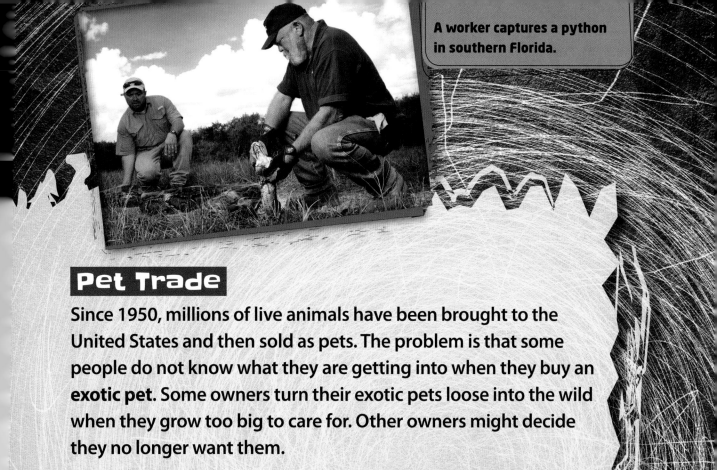

Pet Trade

Since 1950, millions of live animals have been brought to the United States and then sold as pets. The problem is that some people do not know what they are getting into when they buy an **exotic pet**. Some owners turn their exotic pets loose into the wild when they grow too big to care for. Other owners might decide they no longer want them.

For example, giant snakes called pythons were brought to Florida as pets. Their owners, however, had no idea how big the pythons would become, so they released them. Because they have no natural enemies, these invaders multiplied and spread rapidly. Now they are a tremendous menace in Florida. They scare people, eat native animals, and take over habitats of native species.

Some owners of exotic fish empty their fish tanks into storm drains. These fish can survive, reach open water, and compete with native fish for food.

Other exotic animals might escape from their cages. If they survive, the animals can become invasive species.

Thousands of exotic birds are let loose each year in the United States.

9

Ship Traffic

Ships carry many of the products we use in daily life. They sail to a port and deliver their goods. At the same time, a ship can unload invasive species without knowing it. The hitchhikers hide in the ballast tanks that are filled with water to balance the cargo.

Every day cargo container ships pull in water from one port and dump it in another. Hundreds of species are transported from one habitat to the next in this way. When they arrive, they try to take the food and shelter from animals where they land.

A cargo container ship empties its bilges during a stop in a foreign port.

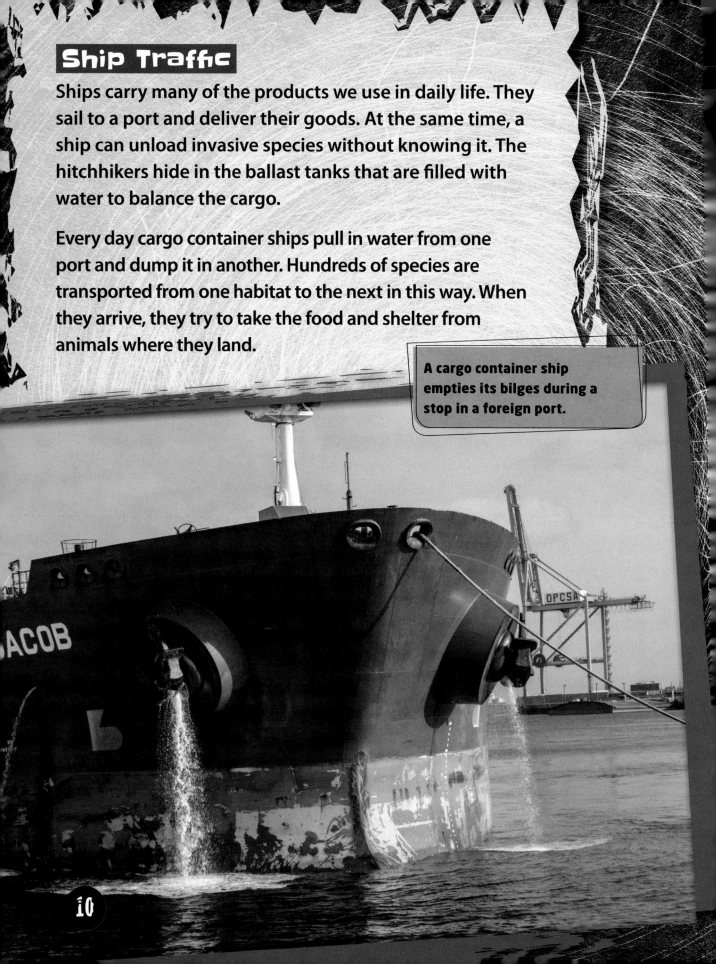

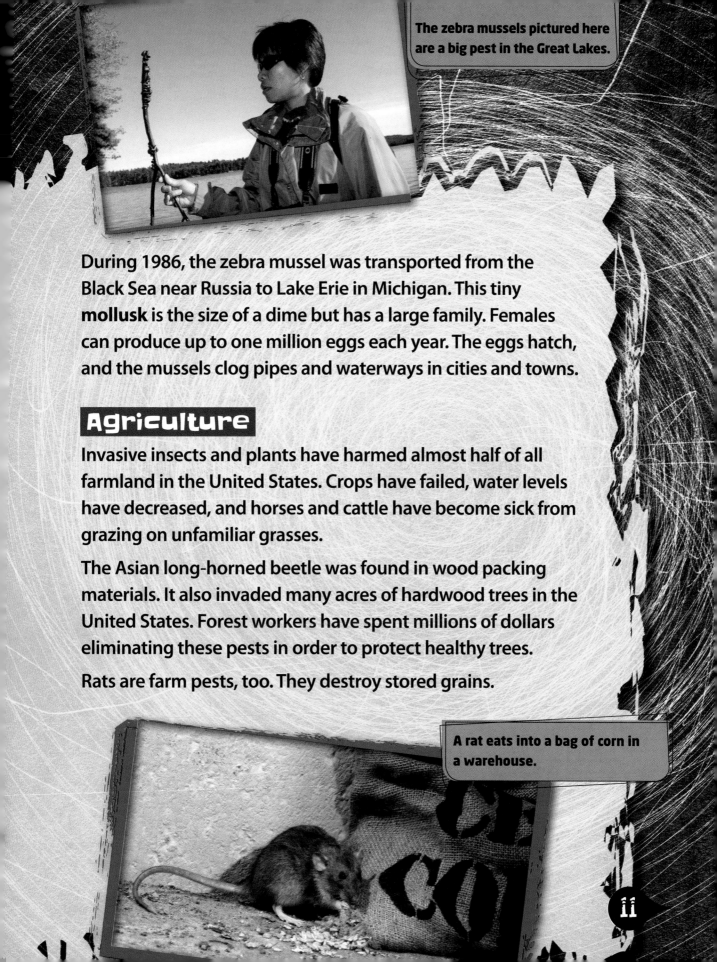

During 1986, the zebra mussel was transported from the Black Sea near Russia to Lake Erie in Michigan. This tiny **mollusk** is the size of a dime but has a large family. Females can produce up to one million eggs each year. The eggs hatch, and the mussels clog pipes and waterways in cities and towns.

Agriculture

Invasive insects and plants have harmed almost half of all farmland in the United States. Crops have failed, water levels have decreased, and horses and cattle have become sick from grazing on unfamiliar grasses.

The Asian long-horned beetle was found in wood packing materials. It also invaded many acres of hardwood trees in the United States. Forest workers have spent millions of dollars eliminating these pests in order to protect healthy trees.

Rats are farm pests, too. They destroy stored grains.

A rat eats into a bag of corn in a warehouse.

Travel and Tourism

Every day, people travel for work and vacation. They often come home with invasive species without knowing it. Small insects can land on their clothing and leave eggs and other organisms. Many of these insects cannot be seen with the human eye. Even the common house mouse can pass on disease to hunters, hikers, and boaters.

Invasive species also affect fishermen. Invasive species of fish and certain types of algae crowd out native species. Fishermen can no longer count on pulling in lake trout, catfish, and yellow perch. This hurts tourism and all those who depend upon it for their livelihoods.

These zebra mussels reproduced so rapidly that they now cover this beach.

Pest Control

Some fruit farmers in the United States and Canada are now spraying their fields to get rid of a pest called the spotted wing drosophila. The drosophila kills cherries and various types of berries, including strawberries. It can also attack fruits such as nectarines and plums. This invasive pest can ruin fruit orchards in a very short period of time and is a serious threat to farmers. However, some chemicals that farmers use to kill drosophila also kill beneficial plants and animals.

In 1907, in order to stop the spread of invasive rabbits, the government of Australia built a fence hundreds of miles long. The fence did not work because it was too hard to maintain. The rabbits thrived, causing serious environmental damage. The rabbits also cause millions of dollars in agricultural damage each year.

Boars were brought from Europe to the United States. Farmers wanted them to kill snakes, but that turned out to be a bad idea. Unfortunately, the European boars mated with California pigs. Their offspring became wild, or feral. Feral boars eat almost anything. They destroy crops. They can eat their way across a field of fresh vegetables in no time.

Wild boars now live in every part of California. Their numbers grew so fast that they became an invasive species.

Ladybugs and their larvae are good natural pest controllers. They eat large numbers of aphids—very destructive pests that feed on plants. There is, however, one species of ladybug that is not so helpful. The squash ladybug eats the leaves of beans, potatoes, and grains. Left unchecked, these ladybugs can become pests.

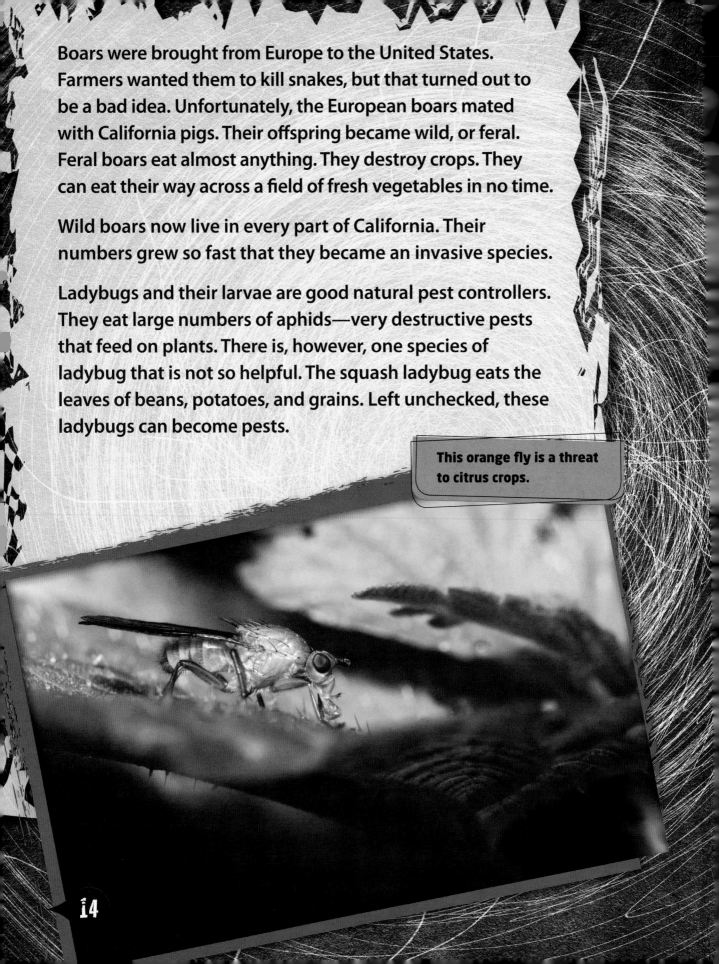

This orange fly is a threat to citrus crops.

Mosquitoes carry diseases that harm millions each year.

Immediate Consequences of Invasion

Invasive Species Spread Disease

Nine people became sick from the **hantavirus** in Yosemite National Park in 2012. Deer mice pass on this disease. People near the mice got sick. Some people have died from the virus.

Mosquitoes spread yellow fever and malaria, and infected birds from Africa brought West Nile virus to North America. People infected by this disease get very sick, and some people have died as a result of it. West Nile virus also harms horses and reptiles such as crocodiles.

This deer mouse can carry a deadly disease, hantavirus.

Invasive Species Disturb Habitats

Wild invaders move across the world by sea and air and make their home in new lands and in waterways. The sea lamprey, which has made its way from the ocean into the Great Lakes, feeds on many kinds of fish. It attaches itself to another fish with a mouth like a suction cup. Then it saws through the skin with its sharp tongue and teeth. Victims die from blood loss or infection.

Red fire ants came to the United States by accident in 1930. Today, they are an invasive species. They build mounds in rotting logs, under buildings, and in parks, meadows, and farm fields. If you step on a nest, the ants will swarm up your leg and sting.

Red fire ants are gathering food. The sting of the fire ant is very painful.

Invasive Species Steal Food

Invasive animals, insects, and funguses can eat huge amounts of native plants that are food for people and native animals. Deprived of their natural food sources, many native species then starve to death. Invaders also eat species that are too small to fight back.

Some invasive insects make a meal of other insects that are important for pollinating plants.

In the state of Indiana, gypsy moths are destroying forests. The moths were brought to the United States from Europe in the 1800s for research. A jar holding the moths broke, and the moths got loose. They hurt native trees by eating all of their leaves. The trees became weak and died.

Invasive Species Interfere with the Birth of Native Animals

Invasive species do more than steal food and harm habitats. They keep native animals from giving birth to their young. Snakes eat bird eggs and small birds that are too small to defend themselves.

These gypsy moths caterpillars are not native to the United States. They grow up to be pests that strip trees of their leaves.

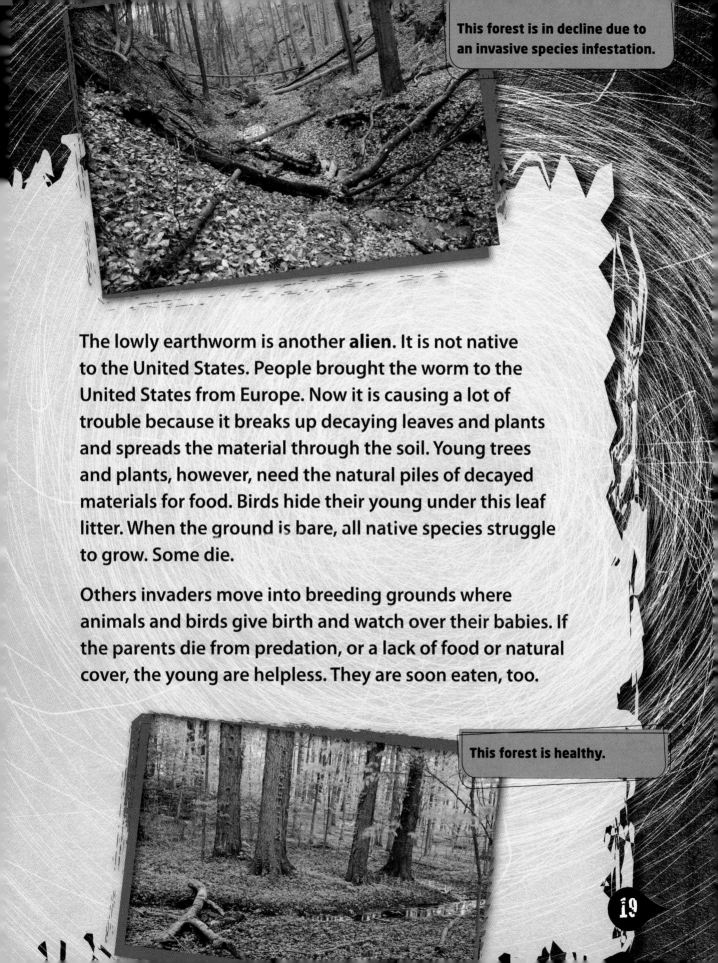

The lowly earthworm is another **alien**. It is not native to the United States. People brought the worm to the United States from Europe. Now it is causing a lot of trouble because it breaks up decaying leaves and plants and spreads the material through the soil. Young trees and plants, however, need the natural piles of decayed materials for food. Birds hide their young under this leaf litter. When the ground is bare, all native species struggle to grow. Some die.

Others invaders move into breeding grounds where animals and birds give birth and watch over their babies. If the parents die from predation, or a lack of food or natural cover, the young are helpless. They are soon eaten, too.

This forest is healthy.

Future Consequences of Invasion

Ecosystems Are Changed

What happens when an invader takes over the natural habitat of another animal? Native plants and animals get out of balance. Nature groups formed by concerned citizens try to bring back balance. They may introduce a predator to stop the invasive species. If they do not control the predator, it may become an invasive species, too.

Horses, sheep, goats, and pigs are farm animals. If, however, they run away from their homes, they often find and take over new habitats in their search for food. If no predators eat them, they grow in number. Then they become pests and change the **ecosystem**.

This Nile monitor is an invader.

A herd of feral hogs are rooting for food.

Spanish explorers brought pigs to the Americas in the 1500s. Some pigs escaped and became feral. Feral pigs reproduced rapidly, and over hundreds of years, they spread to 45 states.

In Michigan, feral pigs are a huge problem. They carry diseases that harm wildlife, eat native species, and give birth to huge litters. There were no wild pigs in Michigan in the 1970s. Now there are more than 3,000 in the state.

Native Species Are Endangered

Invaders change the land when they move in. Some animals die when invasive species move into their homes. The invaders eat the native species or mate with them. Then they give birth to more invaders. Invaders also harm fisheries and hunting grounds.

The ruddy duck is one such animal. Some were taken from the United States to England in the 1930s. The ducks soon escaped into the wild. The ruddy duck took over the breeding grounds of native English ducks causing them to become an **endangered** species.

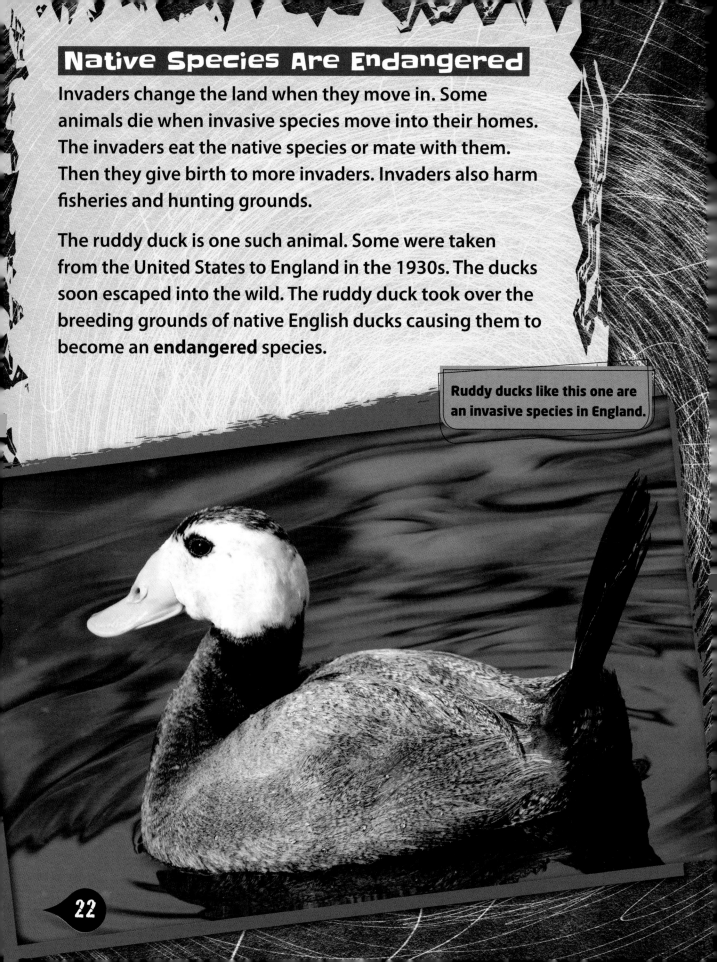

Ruddy ducks like this one are an invasive species in England.

European green crabs, like the one pictured here, are an invasive species to the United States.

Africanized honey bees likes these shown here are dangerous pests.

Invasive Species Replace Native Species

Invasive species drive out native species by taking over their habitats. Birds, rats, fish, and insects that are not native to an area change the balance of nature. Mammals and sea life have a hard time staying alive.

The European green crab is one of these invaders. It preys on clams, oysters, mussels, snails, and other crabs. This invasive species was first discovered in San Francisco Bay on the Pacific coast in 1989. By the turn of the century, it had spread north all the way to British Columbia, probably in the ballast water on ships. The crab creates a large family quickly.

Native Species Are at Risk

More than one quarter of all native birds in North America are in trouble due to invasive species that have taken over their natural habitats.

The brown tree snake is an invasive species in Guam. It has caused 40 species of wild birds to become **extinct**.

Some invasive plant species, like the aggressive kudzu plant, grow so quickly over other plants that they kill them by blocking out the sunlight.

Kudzu is a climbing vine originally from southeast China and southern Japan.

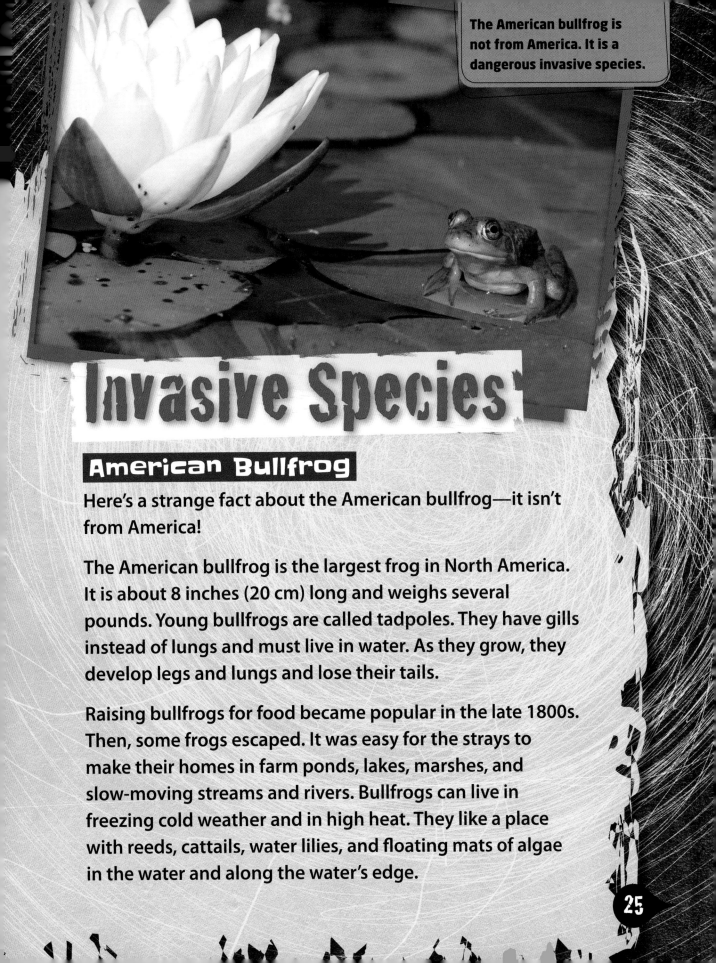

Invasive Species

American Bullfrog

Here's a strange fact about the American bullfrog—it isn't from America!

The American bullfrog is the largest frog in North America. It is about 8 inches (20 cm) long and weighs several pounds. Young bullfrogs are called tadpoles. They have gills instead of lungs and must live in water. As they grow, they develop legs and lungs and lose their tails.

Raising bullfrogs for food became popular in the late 1800s. Then, some frogs escaped. It was easy for the strays to make their homes in farm ponds, lakes, marshes, and slow-moving streams and rivers. Bullfrogs can live in freezing cold weather and in high heat. They like a place with reeds, cattails, water lilies, and floating mats of algae in the water and along the water's edge.

Bullfrogs eat fish, snails, ducklings, snakes, and other small animals. They stuff their large mouths with as much food as their mouths can hold. They also kill and eat native frogs. Female bullfrogs lay between 6,000 and 7,000 eggs at one time. Some lay up to 25,000 eggs! The American bullfrog is one of the worst invasive species in the world.

People add to the problem as well. They capture bullfrogs in the wild and take them home. Many of the frogs are sick and make people, fish, and small animals sick, too.

This American bullfrog is hunting for food. It kills and eats many kinds of native animals.

Cane Toad

The cane toad starts as an egg in a long string of jelly. A female lays between 8,000 and 25,000 eggs at once. The strings of jelly stretch over 60 feet (18 m) in length. Tadpoles hatch within 2 to 7 days. Then, thousands of the tiny black creatures with short tails clump together in groups. The tadpoles develop into toadlets in about 4 weeks. Cane toad eggs, tadpoles, and toadlets are poisonous and can kill animals that eat them.

The adult cane toad measures 4 to 9 inches (10 to 23 cm) long. Its skin has small bumps that look like warts. Behind the toad's ears is a gland that makes a milky liquid that is poisonous to many species. It cannot kill humans, but it can make them sick.

Growers brought the cane toad to Australia in 1935 to eat cane beetles in the sugarcane fields. First, cane toads were given a test. Cane beetles were their only food. The toads ate thousands of them. Farmers were happy to see their large appetites. But when the toads were put into the fields, they started eating the sugarcane too.

Cane toads became an invasive species. Their numbers increased very, very quickly. They took over habitats and stole food from native animals. More than $7 million has been spent trying to control the cane toad.

Cane toads overwhelm native animals.

The cane toad eats insects—which is good. But it also eats sugarcane—which is bad!

Baby boars grow rapidly and are soon on their own.

European Wild Boar

As you have learned, the European wild boar is a member of the wild pig family. Boars live in the forests of Europe, Africa, and Asia. They are medium in size with large heads and front ends. They have long, straight snouts, which give them a keen sense of smell. Their favorite habitat is a forest with broad-leafed trees that provide plenty of food.

Wild boars eat mostly fruits and vegetables. They will, however, eat anything they can stuff into their mouths.

Female boars give birth to four to six piglets in a nest of leaves, grass, and moss. They stay with their babies for 2 weeks to keep them safe. When the piglets are about 7 months old, they are ready to live on their own.

Feral boars are very hard to catch and kill.

29

Spanish explorers brought boars to North America to use as farm pigs. The boars formed wild groups.

These wild hogs harm the ecosystems where they live. They root for food on the forest floor and destroy native plants. They roll around in wetlands and pull up the greens that are food for native wildlife. They destroy breeding sites and make a mess of habitats that were once home to endangered amphibians.

Every year, 20,000 tons (18.1 million kg) of sugarcane alone is lost due to the damage caused by wild boars.

A feral boar eats the roots of native plants.

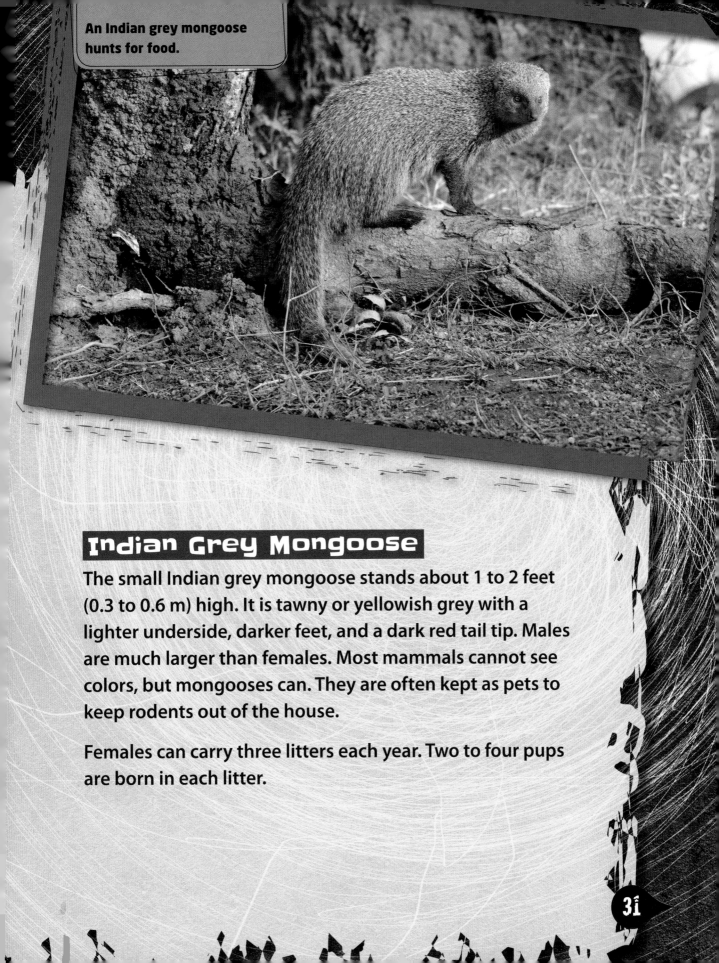

Indian Grey Mongoose

The small Indian grey mongoose stands about 1 to 2 feet (0.3 to 0.6 m) high. It is tawny or yellowish grey with a lighter underside, darker feet, and a dark red tail tip. Males are much larger than females. Most mammals cannot see colors, but mongooses can. They are often kept as pets to keep rodents out of the house.

Females can carry three litters each year. Two to four pups are born in each litter.

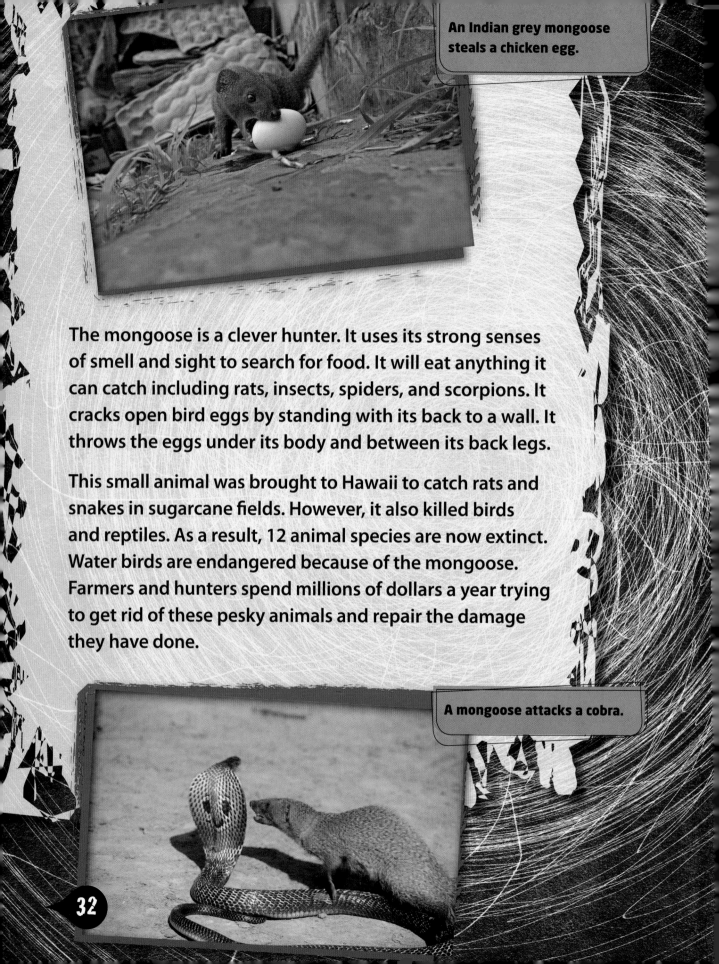

The mongoose is a clever hunter. It uses its strong senses of smell and sight to search for food. It will eat anything it can catch including rats, insects, spiders, and scorpions. It cracks open bird eggs by standing with its back to a wall. It throws the eggs under its body and between its back legs.

This small animal was brought to Hawaii to catch rats and snakes in sugarcane fields. However, it also killed birds and reptiles. As a result, 12 animal species are now extinct. Water birds are endangered because of the mongoose. Farmers and hunters spend millions of dollars a year trying to get rid of these pesky animals and repair the damage they have done.

A mongoose attacks a cobra.

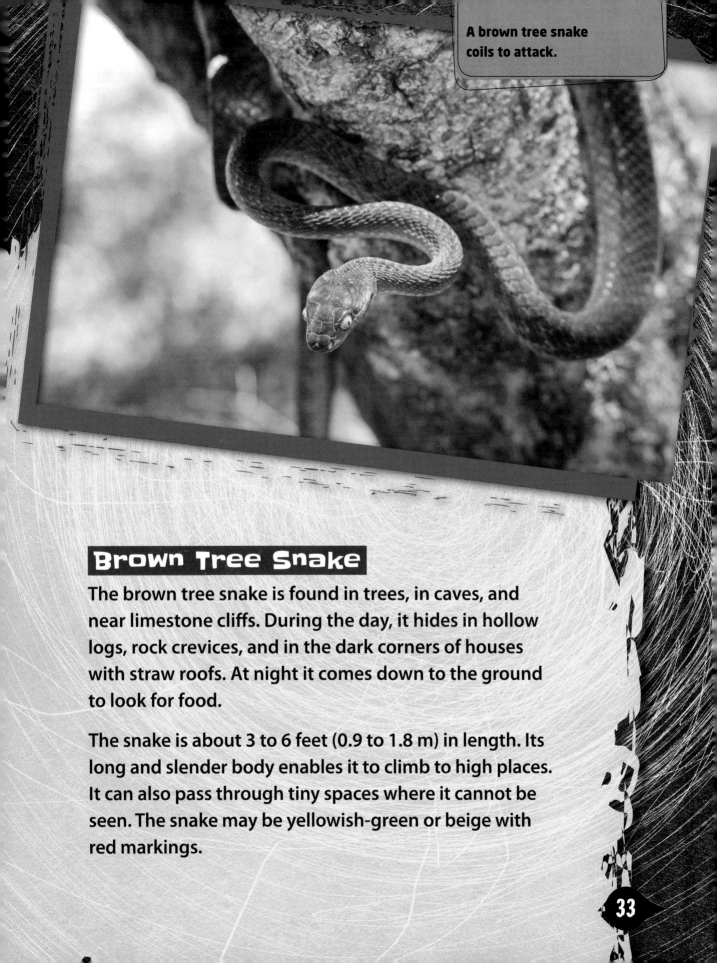

A brown tree snake coils to attack.

Brown Tree Snake

The brown tree snake is found in trees, in caves, and near limestone cliffs. During the day, it hides in hollow logs, rock crevices, and in the dark corners of houses with straw roofs. At night it comes down to the ground to look for food.

The snake is about 3 to 6 feet (0.9 to 1.8 m) in length. Its long and slender body enables it to climb to high places. It can also pass through tiny spaces where it cannot be seen. The snake may be yellowish-green or beige with red markings.

The brown tree snake's native home is Papua New Guinea, an island north of Australia. Some people believe brown tree snakes hitched a ride on military ships going to Guam from Papua New Guinea after World War II. The snakes landed on Guam where there were plenty of lizards and birds for food. Because they have no natural predators on Guam, the brown tree snake population has exploded.

Brown tree snakes can climb a tree in a flash to get to chick eggs and small birds. Ten kinds of birds in Guam are now gone forever. This greedy snake has also wiped out most of Guam's lizard and bat species.

A brown tree snake hunts for food.

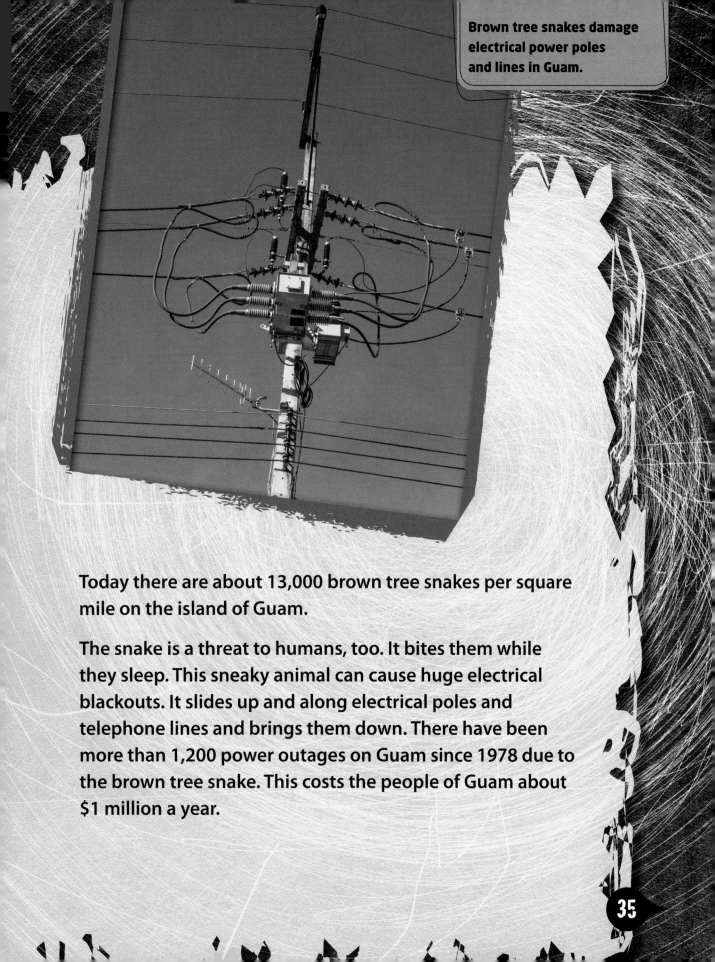

Brown tree snakes damage electrical power poles and lines in Guam.

Today there are about 13,000 brown tree snakes per square mile on the island of Guam.

The snake is a threat to humans, too. It bites them while they sleep. This sneaky animal can cause huge electrical blackouts. It slides up and along electrical poles and telephone lines and brings them down. There have been more than 1,200 power outages on Guam since 1978 due to the brown tree snake. This costs the people of Guam about $1 million a year.

Asian Carp

The Asian carp has many names—grass carp, bighead carp, silver carp, and black carp. These fish were brought to the United States in the 1970s to eat algae from ponds in Arkansas. The fish escaped from the ponds and found their way into rivers. They began swimming up and down the Mississippi River eating plankton and pushing out other species.

An adult Asian carp can weigh 60 to 100 pounds (27 to 45 kg). It will eat anything and live in any body of water. Now it thrives in the Illinois and Mississippi Rivers, which has resulted in a decline in the native fish population.

Asian carp are able to leap out of the water.

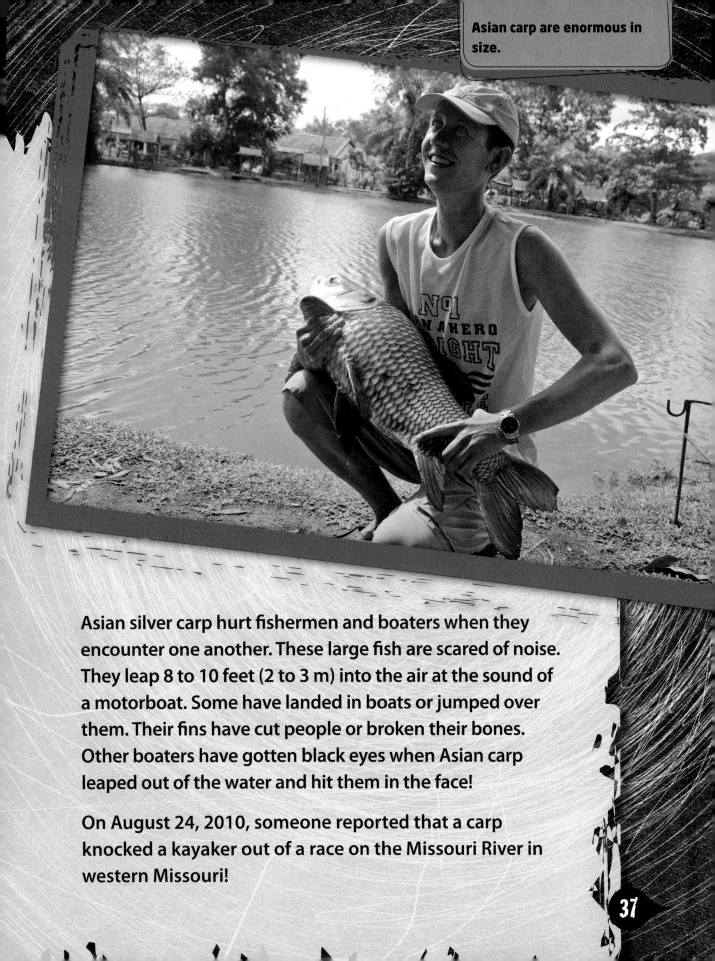

Asian silver carp hurt fishermen and boaters when they encounter one another. These large fish are scared of noise. They leap 8 to 10 feet (2 to 3 m) into the air at the sound of a motorboat. Some have landed in boats or jumped over them. Their fins have cut people or broken their bones. Other boaters have gotten black eyes when Asian carp leaped out of the water and hit them in the face!

On August 24, 2010, someone reported that a carp knocked a kayaker out of a race on the Missouri River in western Missouri!

All Asian carp are invasive. They steal habitats and dig up water plants. Bighead and silver carp take food from paddlefish and clams.

The government has built three electric fences to keep Asian carp out of the Great Lakes. But the fences may not be working. In 2010, a man caught a carp in a river near Lake Michigan.

Asian carp threaten the $7 billion fishery business of the Great Lakes region. They must be stopped before they do even more harm to the environment.

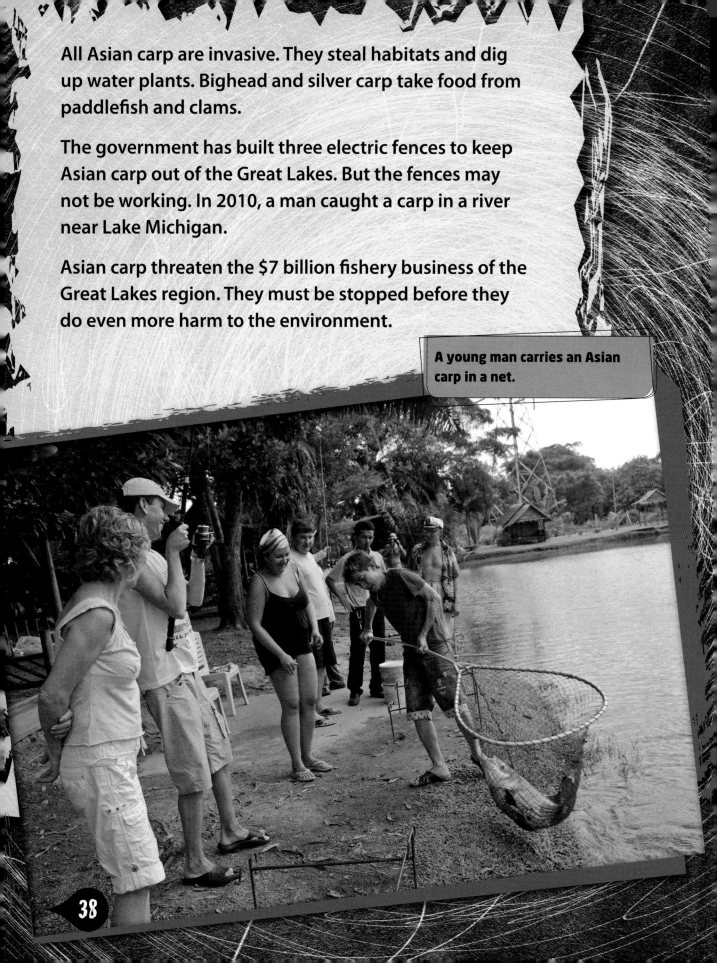

A young man carries an Asian carp in a net.

An adult nutria hunts for food.

Nutria

Nutrias are related to the beaver. They were brought to California at the end of the 19th century to be raised for fur. The fur trade failed and, as a result, many nutria owners turned their animals loose. Then wildlife agencies tried to use nutrias to control weeds. But this wild animal did not stop with weeds. It chewed through areas that were once thick with plants. Nutrias may destroy as much as 40 square miles (103 sq km) of Louisiana's coastal marshes each year.

This animal tears up the nests of birds and small animals. It also harms baby shrimp, crabs, and oysters. Nutrias turn over the soil along the edge of the water. Water then pulls away the top layer of dirt. Plant roots die. It takes a long time to grow new vegetation.

The Blackwater National Wildlife Refuge in Maryland has lost over 8,000 acres (3,235 ha) from nutria damage, and over 50 percent of the remaining marshes are threatened by nutrias. The marshes may or may not recover. There are no natural predators to stop these pests, so they keep spreading into new areas.

A nutria feeds on native plants.

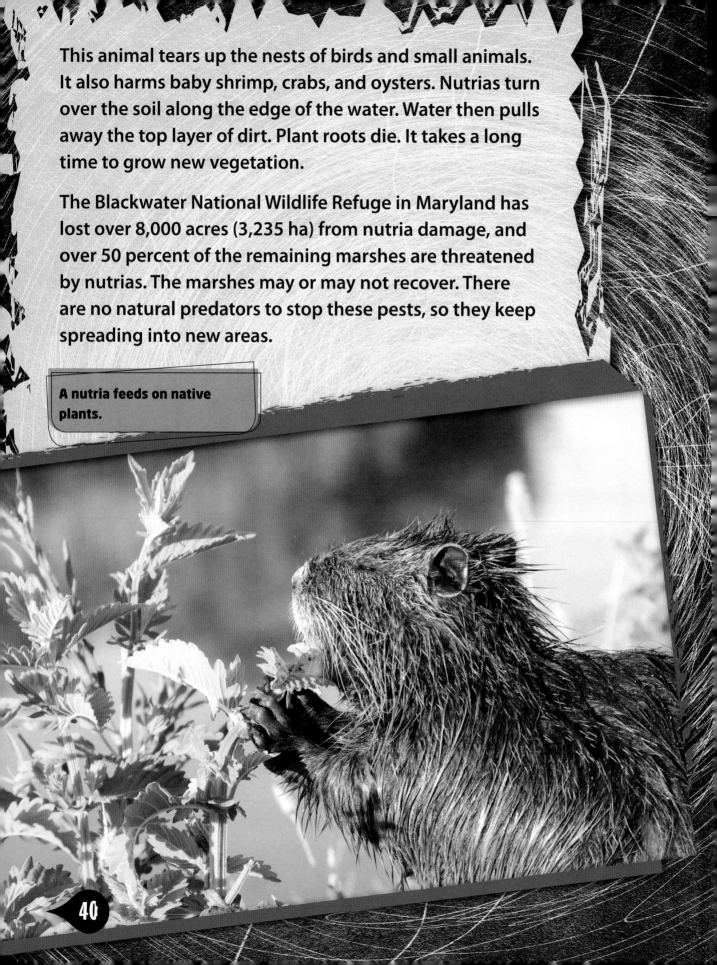

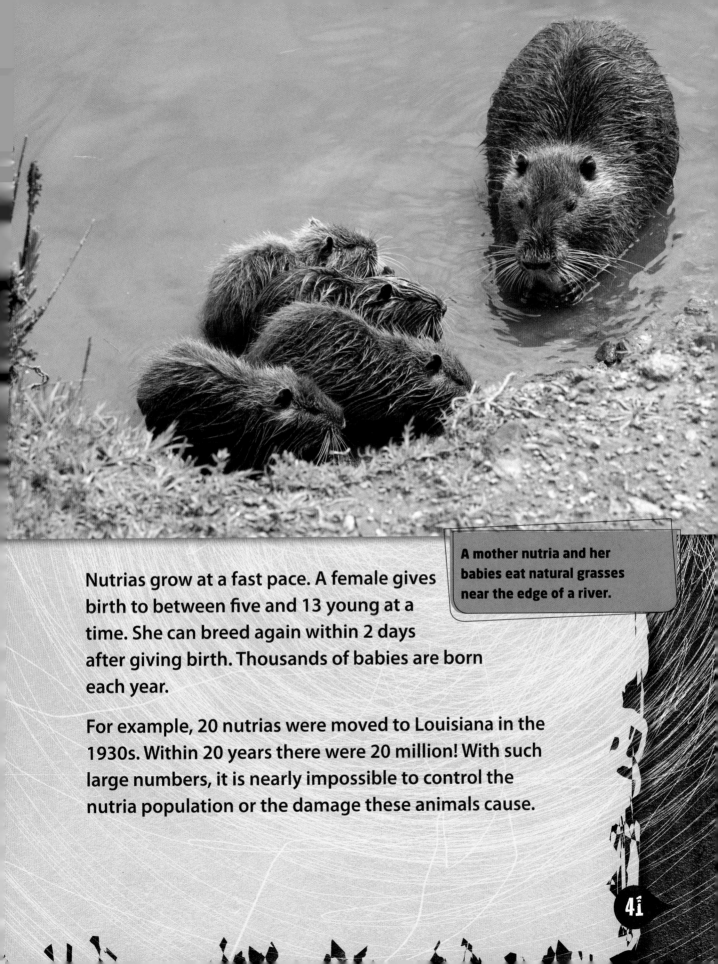

A mother nutria and her babies eat natural grasses near the edge of a river.

Nutrias grow at a fast pace. A female gives birth to between five and 13 young at a time. She can breed again within 2 days after giving birth. Thousands of babies are born each year.

For example, 20 nutrias were moved to Louisiana in the 1930s. Within 20 years there were 20 million! With such large numbers, it is nearly impossible to control the nutria population or the damage these animals cause.

Conservation Efforts

You Can Help

Here are some ways you can help stop the spread of invasive species.

Find out what invasive species may be in or around your community.

Clean your shoes and gear after you go on a hike or nature walk. Check the library for the names of people who can help you learn about the species where you live. If you see an animal or an insect that does not belong, tell someone who can help you report it.

This snail is an invasive species.

All species, even these seagulls, are in danger of losing their homes to invasive species.

Education

You can join a wildlife group. Look on the Internet for the Nature Conservancy and the National Wildlife Federation. Find out how to become a member.

Help spread the word about invasive species. Write a report for school or for your city newspaper. Tell other people about the harm caused by invasive species.

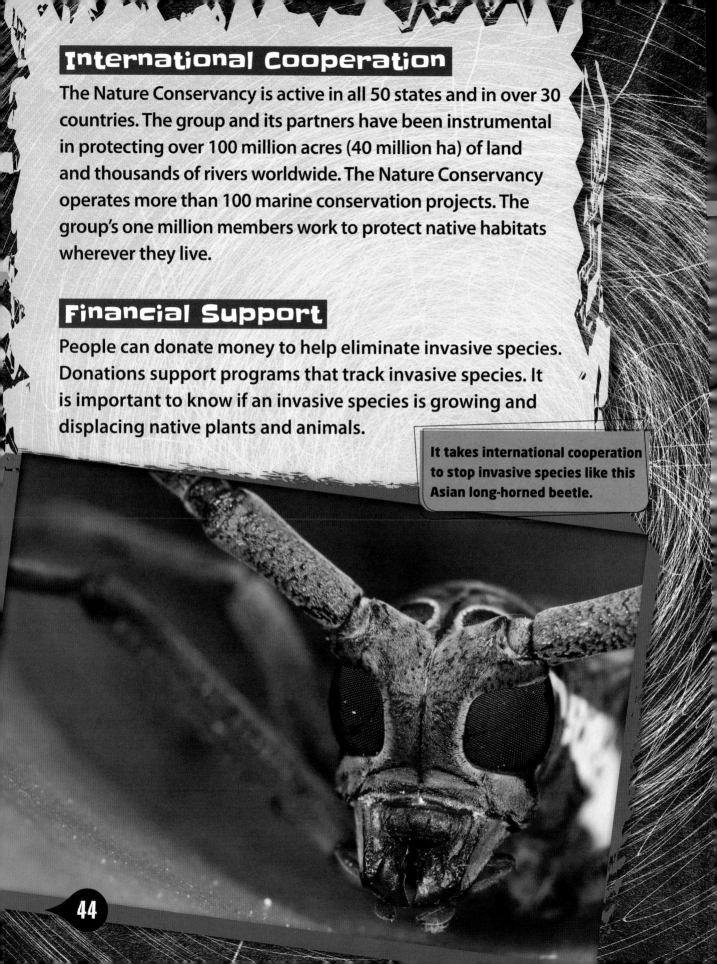

International Cooperation

The Nature Conservancy is active in all 50 states and in over 30 countries. The group and its partners have been instrumental in protecting over 100 million acres (40 million ha) of land and thousands of rivers worldwide. The Nature Conservancy operates more than 100 marine conservation projects. The group's one million members work to protect native habitats wherever they live.

Financial Support

People can donate money to help eliminate invasive species. Donations support programs that track invasive species. It is important to know if an invasive species is growing and displacing native plants and animals.

It takes international cooperation to stop invasive species like this Asian long-horned beetle.

A herd of springbok graze in a field of grass, their natural habitat.

Conclusion

Invasive species cause some native species to go extinct. They have few if any natural predators, and so they dominate the food supply. They cause billions of dollars in damage to crops, farms, and granaries. Plus, some invasive species bring deadly diseases with them that harm animals and humans.

Invasive species are harmful, but there is hope. Many governments have passed laws making it illegal to transport most plants and animals between countries.

The fight against destructive invasive species will be a long one. But if we want to preserve our native habitats and not see native plants and animals go extinct, we must join the fight against invasive species.

Glossary

alien: a species introduced outside its normal distribution

ecosystem: a community of living things and the surroundings in which they live

endangered: in danger of dying out within 20 years

exotic pet: species kept as a pet that is not native to the owner's country

extinct: no longer existing

feral: wild, not domesticated, animals

habitat: the surroundings where an animal or a plant naturally lives

hantavirus: life-threatening disease spread to humans by rodents

invasive species: a kind of animal not native to the ecosystem and whose introduction causes or is likely to cause economic or environmental harm

mollusk: animals with a soft body encased by a shell such as snails, clams, and squids

native species: animals belonging to a particular place by birth

pest: living organisms which are invasive and destructive to plants, animals, ecosystems, and humans or human concerns (livestock and human structures), and may also cause illness

predators: animals that kill other animals for food

species: a single kind of living thing

wildlife: all living things out of the direct control of humans

For More Information

Books

Heckman, Mark and Mark Newman. *Sooper Yooper, Environmental Defender*. San Diego, CA: Thunder Bay Press, 2010.

Metz, Lorijo. *What Can We Do About Invasive Species?* New York, NY: Rosen Publishing, 2009.

Websites

Center for Invasive Species and Ecosystem Health
www.invasive.org/
Provides information and high-quality images about invasive species.

National Invasive Species Information Center (NISIC)
www.invasivespeciesinfo.gov/
NISIC is a gateway to invasive species information covering federal, state, local, and international sources.

Index